Your Baby's BAPTISM

CELEBRATING THE
CHRISTENING
OF A CHILD

DAVID STONE

Illustrated by Chris Molan

HODDER AND STOUGHTON
London Sydney Auckland

For the parents of my godchildren,
Matthew, Samuel, Freddie, Kitty and Laura.

NOTES

THE ADMINISTRATION OF BAPTISM Holy Baptism is normally administered by the parish priest in the course of public worship on Sunday; but it may be administered at other times, and he may delegate its administration to other lawful ministers. Where rubrics indicate that a passage is to be said by 'the priest', this must be understood to include any other minister authorised to administer Holy Baptism.

THE ANSWERING OF THE QUESTIONS When children who are old enough to respond are baptised, the parents and godparents answer the questions (sections 48 and 53, pages 18 and 24), and at the discretion of the priest the children may also answer them.

THE SIGNING WITH THE CROSS The signing with the cross may take place either at section 49 (page 20) or at section 56 (page 24). The sign of the cross may be made in oil blessed for this purpose.

THE GIVING OF A CANDLE A lighted candle, which may be the paschal candle, may be made ready so that other candles may be lighted from it.

THE USE OF THE CANDIDATE'S NAME At the signing with the cross and the giving of a candle, the priest or other minister may address the candidate by name.

THE PEOPLE'S RESPONSES At the signing with the cross it is sufficient if the people join in and say their part (section 49 and 56) once only, when all have been signed; and if a candle is given to those who have been baptised, it is sufficient if the people join in and say their part (section 57, page 26) once only, when all have received a candle.

THE ATTENDANCE OF THE PEOPLE This order of service should normally be used at Holy Communion or Morning or Evening Prayer. At other times representatives of the regular congregation should attend the service, so that they may welcome the newly baptized (section 58, page 26) and be put in mind of their own baptism.

THE ADMINISTRATION OF THE WATER A threefold administration of water (whether by dipping or pouring) is a very ancient practice of the Church, and is commended as testifying to the faith of the Trinity in which candidates are baptized. Nevertheless, a single administration is also lawful and valid.

ALTERNATIVE READINGS Section 45 may be omitted and either Matthew 28.16-20 or John 3.1-8 read in its place.

British Library Cataloguing in Publication Data
A Catalogue Record for this book is available from the British Library
ISBN 0 340 60827 7
Copyright © 1994 by David Stone.
Illustration © 1994 by Christine Molan.

First published in Great Britain 1994.
10 9 8 7 6 5 4 3 2 1

Published by Hodder and Stoughton,
a division of Hodder Headline plc,
338 Euston Road, London NW1 3BH.
Printed in Belgium by Proost International Book Production.

FOREWORD

by the Bishop of London, The Rt Revd and Rt Hon David Hope

Baptism is an occasion for celebration, a time for thanksgiving. It is an important event in the life of any family. Often this is marked by a party, members of the wider family will gather together from all parts of the country, and gifts and cards will be given to the newly baptised child.

Such celebrations are entirely appropriate. As David Stone sets out so well in this book, baptism is a major event, 'nothing less than switching from death to life' (page 7).

It is because the Christian Church does regard baptism as so major an event that a book like this is long overdue. As with so much in the Church, we so easily confuse people with difficult language, or simply do not attempt to explain fully and clearly what is actually happening.

This book will make an ideal gift for all parents who are considering baptism, as well as for those who have decided to have their child baptised. It explains, in clear terms, all the practical steps needed to prepare for a baptism. It also goes through the service itself and tries to make clear the meaning of the various parts of the service, as well as setting out the nature of the commitment to be made by parents and godparents.

I believe that this book will be of enormous benefit to very many people. As stated so clearly in the book, one of the most important aspects of baptism is that it is the beginning of a relationship with God which hopefully will be lifelong. As the child is established in such a relationship and a new beginning is celebrated, it is essential that the Church does all it can to help the family, in particular the parents and godparents, to understand fully the implications of such a decision. David Stone has provided a means by which the baptism service itself will become a real cause of celebration and thanksgiving.

3

CONTENTS

Having a baby is a time of great and glorious upheaval. There are all sorts of changes to be made, especially if the baby is your first. The entire focus of your life shifts as you begin to look after the brand new human being which has been entrusted to you. You'll want to do the very best you can as you care for them.

It's obvious that your new baby relies on you for his or her physical and material needs. What may be less apparent is the way that they depend on you for their spiritual needs as well. And that's where this book comes in. It's designed to guide you in the first few steps of bringing up your child in the Christian faith, especially as you prepare for baptism (or 'christening' as it's sometimes called). Although it's written mainly with the modern Anglican baptism service in mind, it covers themes that are common to many other churches as well. We'll look at what baptism is all about and what you can expect during the service.

Before we get under way, special thanks to Philip Mounstephen, father of Kitty my fourth godchild, for his invaluable comments during the writing of this book.

WHY BRING YOUR BABY
TO BE BAPTISED?

To get the most out of the baptism service, it's important for you to think through this question. People opt for baptism for all sorts of different reasons:

'The Christian faith is very important to us and we want to share this with our baby right from the very beginning.'

Although some churches prefer to let the children make the decision themselves when they grow older, the Church of England has always baptised babies, recognising that it's right for them to be included as members of the Christian family from the word go.

'We want to give our baby the best possible start in life.'

Yes, baptism is a marvellous way of signifying the beginning of a new life. Remember, though, that having a good start is not enough by itself. You need to bring up your child as a follower of Jesus as well. Just as in gardening, it's no good just planting the seeds. The young shoots also need careful nurture to make sure they grow properly. This is why the baptism service stresses the importance of teaching children to become *'faithful in public worship and private prayer, to live by trust in God, and come to confirmation'*.

'Babies in our family have always been christened.'

Yes, but make sure that you yourselves agree with what's going on, and are not simply opting for baptism on the basis of what others say you should do. It helps no one to say that you believe certain things about God if you do not. And it's no good making the solemn promises involved in baptism if you don't really intend to keep them. The Church of England offers a special *Service of Thanksgiving for the Birth of a Child* for parents who don't yet feel ready to go for baptism but would nonetheless like to thank God for their new baby and commit their family to his loving care.

'Babies that aren't baptised don't have God's protection and might not go to heaven if anything happens to them.'

It's true that babies who are very ill are usually baptised in hospital. But we must not think that God would refuse to show his love to a baby simply because he or she has not been baptised. Baptism is good but it isn't a lucky charm or inoculation against things going wrong.

'Baptism is when our baby will be officially named.'

This used to be the case and it explains why we have what we call 'Christian' names. But nowadays, although the baby is addressed by name in baptism, the official naming of a baby is something you do when you give the details of the birth at your local registry office.

'If we don't have our baby baptised, he or she won't be able to get married in church.'

This is no longer the case. Although it's desirable to be a Christian believer when getting married in church, you don't have to have been baptised.

WHAT IS BAPTISM?

Imagine a friend of yours starts a new job. At the end of the day, they stagger back exhausted. 'How did it go?' you ask sympathetically. 'It was awful,' comes the reply. 'The personnel department forgot I was coming, I had no time for lunch, the photocopier broke down, and the coffee machine ran out of sugar!'

You might say that your friend has had a 'baptism of fire'. Apart from quaint expressions like this, we don't talk about baptism very much in everyday life. But your friend's experience actually conveys the two main ideas behind baptism rather well.

First of all, baptism is to do with being overwhelmed. Now Christian baptism is a rather more positive experience than having a disastrous first day in a new job! But at least this illustration gets across the idea that to baptise is to plunge someone right into something. Given our climate and the tendency for churches to be on the chilly side, we tend to be rather more sedate about baptising babies. Rather than immersing them completely, we usually just sprinkle water on to the baby's head. But the symbolism is still there. To baptise someone is, so to speak, to throw them in at the deep end! It needs to be such a dramatic action because it stands for such a drastic change. In spiritual terms, it's nothing less than switching from death to life.

Secondly, baptism is to do with beginnings. Your friend can only have a 'baptism of fire' on the *first* day of a new job. In the same way, Christian baptism marks the *start* of something new. It's the sign that someone has begun the Christian life and become a brand new member of the Christian family.

WHERE DOES BAPTISM COME FROM?

For Christians, baptism goes back about two thousand years, to just before Jesus came on the scene. His cousin John was so into it that he became known as John the *Baptiser* or *Baptist*.

Why was he so keen? John was a preacher. As he spoke to the crowds that came to hear him, he showed them the contrast between their lives as they were and their lives as God wanted them to be. He warned them that God would judge them and urged them to seek forgiveness for the wrongs of the past.

John's hearers were so struck by what he had to say that they wanted to wipe the slate clean there and then. This is where baptism came in. By being baptised, that is, being immersed in the water of the nearby River Jordan, people showed publicly and dramatically their desire to be washed from their sin and to turn over a new leaf for the future.

Jesus took up the same idea. Except that he added an important dimension. Just as John had predicted he would: 'I baptise you with water for repentance,' he said. 'But after me will come one who is more powerful than I ... He will baptise you with the Holy Spirit and with fire.'

What John meant was this. His baptism, using water, helped people express their desire to turn over a new leaf. But, just like the publicity which precedes the release of a new film, he was only the trailer. The main picture was still to come. For Jesus would bring the complete package. His baptism, with the Holy Spirit, would change people on the inside. It would give them the ability to live a new life, not just turn over a new leaf.

Baptism is something that happens to someone on the *outside* (being dipped in or sprinkled with water) as a symbol or sign of something happening on the *inside* (repentance, forgiveness, and the gift of the Holy Spirit). That's what people mean, by the way, when they call baptism a *'sacrament'*: something ordinary which has a special 'sacred' or holy meaning.

The practice of baptising the children of Christian parents is certainly hinted at in the New Testament, and has been the Church's practice from earliest times. We baptise in obedience to what Matthew's Gospel records as the last statement made by Jesus before he returned to heaven: 'All authority in

heaven and on earth has been given to me. Therefore go and make disciples of all nations, baptising them in the name of the Father and of the Son and of the Holy Spirit and teaching them to obey everything I have commanded you. And surely I am with you always, to the very end of the age.'

These days, baptism usually takes place during one of the main Sunday services. This is good, because it emphasises the role the whole church family has in welcoming a new member, and it allows everyone to share in the joy of the event.

PLANNING YOUR BABY'S BAPTISM

If, after reading this book, and thinking and talking it through, you decide that you would like to bring your baby for baptism, here are some of the practical steps to take.

Where can I have my baby baptised?

Baptism will normally take place in your local parish church, either the one in the parish where you live or the one you regularly attend. Sometimes people want their babies baptised elsewhere (in the church where they were married, for example). This is allowed, as long as the clergy of both the parish where you live and the parish where you want the baptism to take place agree.

How do I apply for baptism?

Make an appointment to see your church minister. Ring up or pop round to see them. Many churches advertise a special time when clergy are available to discuss matters like this. Don't plan a date until you've done this. He or she will usually want to spend some time with you to make sure that you understand what baptism is all about and that you're ready to make the commitment involved. Some churches run special baptism preparation groups which you may be invited to attend.

What does it cost?

Nothing. Baptism is absolutely free, though a charge may be made for the baptism certificate. You should keep this in a safe place, as its details will be needed when arrangements are being made for confirmation in the future.

What should your baby wear?

It's up to you. Some families have a traditional christening gown which has been passed down through the family. White is often worn as a symbol of purity. But the most important thing is that your baby is warm and comfortable. Make sure that your baby's hat is removed for the baptism itself!

CHOOSING GODPARENTS

The baptism service makes it clear that prayer, example and teaching are the main areas where parents need the help and support of godparents (sometimes called 'sponsors'). That's why it makes sense for you to choose godparents with these three things uppermost in your mind. It's not a question of whether they'll be able to buy expensive presents or look after your child if anything happens to you. But will they pray for you and your child? Will they set her a good example? Will their teaching be positive, and good for him?

It's usual to choose three godparents, two men and one woman for a boy, and two women and one man for a girl. But you can have more than three if you want to. Church rules also allow parents to be godparents to their own children. Godparents should be both baptised and confirmed, though the requirement of confirmation can be relaxed if the minister agrees. It's usual for godparents to be at the baptism service in person. But if they can't, it's OK for someone to stand in for them.

BAPTISM IN THE ANGLICAN CHURCH

A s a sign that someone is turning away from sin and intends to follow Jesus Christ, baptism may seem at first to be a rather strange thing to do to a little baby. How can babies express that sort of desire? The answer is that they can't. Perhaps, then, we should delay baptism until they can? This is the position taken up by those Christian churches and individuals who leave baptism until children are old enough to make the decision for themselves. In the Church of England, parents who take this view can if they wish opt for the *Service of Thanksgiving for the Birth of a Child* rather than the baptism service.

But baptism is also the badge of belonging to the family of the Christian Church. It's the mark of initiation. It's the sign that someone belongs to Christ (which is why baptism is also known as 'christening'). It doesn't seem right to exclude babies and very young children from the Christian family just because they can't yet understand what's going on. Therefore most churches, including the Anglican Church, baptise babies.

But as the service points out, baptism is not much good on its own. It's just the beginning. Children are baptised *'on the understanding that they are brought up as Christians within the family of the Church'*. So this is how the service begins: by asking parents and godparents to declare publicly that they are willing to do this.

THE DUTIES OF PARENTS AND GODPARENTS

42   The priest says

> Children who are too young to profess the Christian faith are baptized on the understanding that they are brought up as Christians within the family of the Church.
>
> As they grow up, they need the help and encouragement of that family, so that they learn to be faithful in public worship and private prayer, to live by trust in God, and come to confirmation.
>
> Parents and godparents, the *children* whom you have brought for baptism *depend* chiefly on you for the help and encouragement *they need*. Are you willing to give it to *them* by your prayers, by your example, and by your teaching?

Parents and godparents

I am willing.

43   And if the *child* is old enough to understand, the priest speaks to *him* in these or similar words.

> *N*, when you are baptized, you become *a member* of a new family. God takes you for his own *child*, and all Christian people will be your brothers and sisters.

PRAYER, EXAMPLE AND TEACHING

Three things are mentioned as the special responsibilities of parents and godparents.

1 *You're asked to pray for your children.* This is good news. It means that God doesn't expect you to bring up your child all by yourself. It's a partnership between you as their earthly parents and God as their heavenly Father. Praying is a marvellous way of inviting God to help you in the responsibility he has given you for looking after this new life. See pages 28-29 for some specific suggestions.

2 *You're asked to set them a good example.* It can be embarrassing just how much children copy their parents! As your children see how important the Christian faith is to you, they'll be much more likely to take it on board for themselves.

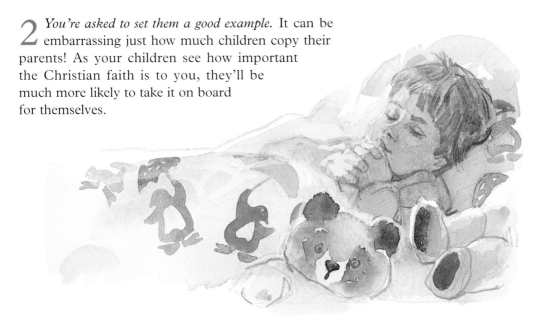

3 *You're asked to teach them.* Notice that this comes *after* setting them a good example! Bringing children up as Christians isn't *all* talk, but it does include teaching them what is true, especially where God is concerned, and how to put Christian belief into practice.

This is a tall order. And that's why you're asked to agree to bring your child up *'within the family of the Church'*. The idea is that the life of the local church should help you in the exciting but exacting job which God has given you as parents: to bring up your child to know and follow him. So if you're not one already, do become a regular member of your local church and use every opportunity for your family to grow and develop in the Christian faith.

Later on, confirmation will give your child the opportunity to 'confirm' that, yes, they want to stand by the promises made on their behalf when they were baptised. Until then, it's mainly up to you!

THE MINISTRY OF THE WORD

Sections 44, 45, and 46 may be omitted when Baptism is administered at
Holy Communion or at Morning or Evening Prayer.

44   Priest   The Lord is loving to everyone;
     All   **and his mercy is over all his works.**

45   Priest

God is the creator of all things, and by the birth of children he gives to parents
a share in the work and joy of creation. But we who are born of earthly parents
need to be born again. For in the Gospel Jesus tells us that unless a man has
been born again, he cannot see the Kingdom of God. And so God gives us the
way to a second birth, a new creation and life in union with him.

Baptism is the sign and seal of this new birth. In St Matthew's Gospel we read
of the risen Christ commanding his followers to make disciples of all nations
and to baptize men everywhere; and in the Acts of the Apostles we read of St
Peter preaching in these words: 'Repent and be baptized in the name of Jesus
Christ for the forgiveness of sins; and you shall receive the gift of the Holy
Spirit. For the promise is to you and your children and to all that are afar off,
everyone whom the Lord calls to him.'

In obedience to this same command we ourselves were baptized and now
bring *these children* to baptism.

46   Priest   We thank God therefore for our baptism to life in Christ, and we
                pray for *these children (N)* and say together
     All   **Heavenly Father, in your love**
                you have called us to know you,
                led us to trust you,
                and bound our life with yours.
                Surround *these children* **with your love;**
                protect *them* **from evil;**
                fill *them* **with your Holy Spirit;**
                and receive *them* **into the family of your Church;**
                that *they* **may walk with us in the way of Christ**
                and grow in the knowledge of your love. Amen.

THE MEANING OF BAPTISM

NEW BIRTH

After all the effort involved in the last few months of being pregnant and the trauma of giving birth, we might be tempted to think that that was that! But no. According to Jesus, physical birth is not enough. You can read what he had to say in the third chapter of John's Gospel. The basic message is that we human beings need to be born again, born *spiritually*. Otherwise, Jesus warned, we cannot see the kingdom of God.

What he meant was this. One day God is going to step in and rid our world of all the evil that contaminates and spoils it. One day he will finally answer what we pray in the Lord's Prayer about 'Thy kingdom come, Thy will be done'. He has promised to establish *his* rule, *his* kingdom, to replace the rule of evil and selfishness.

DANGER: CONTAMINATION!

Think of our world as a hospital operating theatre which has become contaminated by a dangerous germ. There's nothing for it: the whole place has got to be thoroughly sterilised. Everything that has been infected must be taken away and destroyed before the theatre can be used again. According to Jesus, this is how God sees our world: fatally flawed and fit only for disposal. The problem is that this includes *us*: for we too are contaminated. This is what the Bible means by '*sin*'. It's not just the wrong things we do: they're merely the tip of the iceberg. No, the real problem is the underlying selfishness that so often makes us do what's wrong and stops us from doing what's right.

The problem is that our innermost selves are firmly biased in favour of self and what *we* want, rather than God and what *he* wants. As you'll soon discover with your own child, human beings don't need to be taught this: the 'me first' compulsion is an inborn thing in all of us. It's this that leads to so much of the evil in our world. The result is that, along with everything else, we too are due for the scrap-heap. God can't take the risk of spoiling heaven by having the likes of us around. And so the only way to survive, the only way, as Jesus puts it, to 'see the kingdom of God', is to make a fresh start, to be born again.

GOOD NEWS!

The good news is that what we need, God gives. There is a way of being cleaned up and decontaminated before God brings down the final curtain. Here's how one of the most famous verses in the Bible puts it: 'For God so loved the world that he gave his one and only Son, that whoever believes in him shall not perish but have eternal life.' What does this mean?

This verse starts with the immense love of God. He has never intended that we should 'perish' or cease to exist when our bodies die. He wants us to enjoy his gift of life for ever. But, like that fatal contamination, our sin has spoiled everything. So God did something about it. He gave his one and only Son to take away the sin of the world – the sins of each one of us.

An incident which made the news a few years ago illustrates this. A group of Venture Scouts were out climbing. As the weather worsened, three boys became separated from the rest of their party. Two experienced climbers, Michael Rudall and Daryl Campling, set out to find them. They were discovered 3000 feet down a steep slope, but just as their rescuers reached them, a rock-fall began higher up the mountainside. Michael Rudall flung his body over one of the young scouts and was killed instantly as the rocks came crashing down.

That climber died to save the boy. His sacrifice is a good picture of what Jesus did in giving his life for us. He died so that we could make a fresh start. The result, for those who believe in him, is forgiveness, decontamination, a new birth and life with God in heaven for ever.

BELIEVING IN JESUS

All these good things are for those who believe in Jesus. So what does it mean to believe? How do we do it?

Imagine that you're feeling a bit under the weather and so you make an appointment to see your doctor. She asks a few questions, prods you about a bit and then sits you down. 'I'm afraid it's bad news ...' How you react to what she says depends on whether or not you believe in her as your doctor. If you do, then you'll agree with her diagnosis and accept whatever radical treatment she recommends. If you don't, then you'll go off and either ignore what she says or seek a second opinion.

Notice that believing in your doctor like this doesn't just mean believing that she *is* a doctor. Yes, you do need to know that she's properly qualified. But that doesn't cure you. To believe in her fully means trusting her diagnosis and doing what she says.

It's the same with believing in Jesus. It's not enough simply to believe the fact that he is the Son of God who has dealt with the problem of the world's sin. Just accepting the truth that he's uniquely qualified to save us won't do. No, to believe in Jesus fully is to trust him and let these things become true for us personally.

In other words, we must accept the diagnosis he offers that the basic problem is our sin, our rebellion against God. We must turn from everything we know to be wrong. We must accept that through his death on the cross Jesus has made it possible for our sin and selfishness to be forgiven. We must receive the treatment and change in lifestyle he prescribes by determining, with the help of his Holy Spirit, to follow him in the future.

Changing our allegiance like this, being forgiven and receiving the Holy Spirit, is what goes on *inside* us. Baptism is the *outward* sign that the inner reality has taken place – or, in the case of babies and young children, it's the outward sign of what we trust will take place as they are brought up in the family of the Church.

This is one of the things we go on to pray for at this point in the service: that, as they grow up, the children we bring to baptism may indeed come to know and experience these important changes of which their baptism is the outward sign.

THE DECISION

47 The parents and godparents stand, and the priest says to them

> Those who bring children to be baptized must affirm their allegiance to Christ and their rejection of all that is evil.

> It is your duty to bring up *these children* to fight against evil and to follow Christ.

48 Therefore I ask these questions which you must answer for yourselves and for *these children*.

> Do you turn to Christ?

Answer **I turn to Christ.**

> Do you repent of your sins?

Answer **I repent of my sins.**

> Do you renounce evil?

Answer **I renounce evil.**

CHANGING SIDES

This is the moment of commitment. As parents and godparents you are asked three questions which you answer for yourself and also on behalf of the child you bring to baptism. They're basically different ways of saying the same thing, inviting you to declare publicly the fact that you have crossed over from 'death' to 'life' - that you have been washed from your sins and have become a follower of Jesus.

1 *Do you turn to Christ?* In other words, what is your attitude to Jesus Christ? Have you stopped living your life for yourself and turned to him?

2 *Do you repent of your sins?* What is your attitude to the things in your life that you know to be wrong and less than God's best for you? Are you prepared to admit that they are there and that they matter? Do you turn away from them?

3 *Do you renounce evil?* What is your attitude to evil? Are you a bit neutral about the things that hurt God and make him angry? Or is evil something you want nothing more to do with?

49   Either here or at Section 56 the priest makes THE SIGN OF THE CROSS on the forehead of each child, saying to each

> I sign you with the cross, the sign of Christ.

After the signing of each or all, he says

> Do not be ashamed to confess the faith of Christ crucified.
>
> **All**   **Fight valiantly under the banner of Christ**
> **against sin, the world, and the devil,**
> **and continue his faithful** *soldiers* **and** *servants*
> **to the end of your** *lives.*

50   Priest   May almighty God deliver you from the powers of darkness, and lead you in the light and obedience of Christ. **Amen.**

51   A HYMN or PSALM may be sung.

MARKED FOR LIFE

I f a new religion were to begin today and take as its symbol a pistol or an electric chair, we would think it very odd. And yet that is effectively what Christianity did. Since earliest times, its emblem has been an instrument of brutal execution and cruel torture: the cross.

Why, then, do we make the sign of a cross on a baby in the baptism service? The answer is that, as the minister says, the cross is the '*sign of Christ*'. Like a badge, the cross marks us out as those who belong to Christ as his followers. It signifies that just as he was ready to put himself in second place, so are we. It says that just as he was willing to give up even his life for others, so are we. That's why the minister goes on: '*Do not be ashamed to confess the faith of Christ crucified.*' Then everyone joins in: '*Fight valiantly under the banner of Christ against sin, the world, and the devil, and continue his faithful soldier and servant to the end of your life.*'

It seems strange to encourage a young baby to fight in a battle. In doing so we acknowledge the reality of evil, not simply as an unpleasant force, but also as a personal enemy. That's why the minister goes on to pray that the baby may be kept safe from the '*powers of darkness*' and be helped to follow Christ.

52   The priest stands before the water of baptism and says

Praise God who made heaven and earth,

All   **who keeps his promise for ever.**

Priest   Almighty God, whose Son Jesus Christ
was baptized in the river Jordan:
we thank you for the gift of water
to cleanse us and revive us;
we thank you that through the waters of the
Red Sea, you led your people out of slavery
to freedom in the promised land;
we thank you that through the deep waters
of death you brought your Son, and raised
him to life in triumph.
Bless this water, that *your servants* who *are*
washed in it may be made one with Christ
in his death and in his resurrection,
to be cleansed and delivered from all sin.
Send your Holy Spirit upon *them* to bring
them to new birth in the family of your
Church, and raise *them* with Christ
to full and eternal life.
For all might, majesty, authority, and power
are yours, now and for ever. **Amen.**

THE SYMBOLISM OF WATER

JESUS WAS BAPTISED

In this prayer we remind ourselves that Jesus himself was baptised. In his Gospel, Matthew tells us that John wasn't too keen at first. He couldn't see why Jesus needed to be baptised. What sins had he ever committed? But Jesus insisted. And so he was baptised *as if* he was as guilty as the rest of humanity. That's how he showed his willingness to be identified with us, to share our pains, to shoulder our burdens. Because he was prepared to be one with us, we can be one with him.

Next we're reminded of two Bible passages where water is an important theme.

THE WATERS OF THE RED SEA

This is a reference to events described in the Old Testament book of Exodus. The people of Israel were in deep trouble. They had languished as slaves in Egypt for many years. Finally, under the leadership of Moses, they were allowed to leave the country and head for freedom. Or so they thought. The problem was that Pharaoh, the head man in Egypt, having let them go, realised how useful it was to have foreign slaves around the place. So he changed his mind and sent an army to bring them back. The soldiers caught up with them just as they reached the Red Sea. With water in front and warriors behind, all seemed lost. Until God miraculously intervened by causing the Sea to part. The Israelites crossed over safely, and then, just as the Egyptian army was on its way over, the waters came back.

This journey from slavery to freedom through the water is a dramatic picture of what happens when someone becomes a Christian, which, as we've seen, is what baptism signifies.

THE DEEP WATERS OF DEATH

This brings us to the next part of the prayer. Death has often been thought of as a river we have to cross. The problem is that we're out of our depth. It's an enemy we can't defeat. Like great weights, our sins drag us down and pull us under. Paul writes about the link between sin and death like this in his letter to the Romans: 'the wages of sin is death...' Not just physical death, but spiritual death too: the ultimate destruction prescribed for everything that spoils and contaminates God's world.

But there is one person in history who was dragged down, not by the weight of his own sin, but by the weight of everyone else's. And so, as the Acts of the Apostles tells us, he didn't stay dead: 'God raised him from the dead, freeing him from the agony of death, because it was impossible for death to keep its hold on him.'

As Jesus was raised to life again, so are we. For along with him come all those who are holding on to him, who believe and trust in him.

So the act of being plunged into the water and coming up again is a picture of our death and resurrection. This is most clearly seen in adult baptism, where the person is physically dipped under the surface of the water. But the idea is still there in the use of the water in the baptism of babies.

53   The priest says to the parents and godparents

> You have brought *these children* to baptism. You must now declare before God and his Church the Christian faith into which *they are* to be baptized, and in which you will help *them* to grow. You must answer for yourselves and for *these children*.
>
> Do you believe and trust in God the Father,
> who made the world?

Answer **I believe and trust in him.**

> Do you believe and trust in his Son Jesus Christ,
> who redeemed mankind?

Answer **I believe and trust in him.**

> Do you believe and trust in his Holy Spirit,
> who gives life to the people of God?

Answer **I believe and trust in him.**

54   The priest turns to the congregation and says

> This is the faith of the Church.

All   **This is our faith.**
        We believe and trust in one God,
        Father, Son, and Holy Spirit.

THE BAPTISM

55   The parents and godparents being present with each child, the priest baptizes *him*. He dips *him* in the water or pours water on *him*, addressing *him* by name.

> *N*, I baptize you in the name of the Father,
> and of the Son, and of the Holy Spirit.

And each one of *his* sponsors answers

Amen.

56   The priest makes THE SIGN OF THE CROSS on the forehead of each child if he has not already done so. The appropriate words are printed at section 49.

THE CHRISTIAN FAITH DECLARED

Christianity is about a new relationship with God in the family of the Church. But which God? And what is he like? This is what we come to next, as parents and godparents declare publicly that the faith the baby is being baptised into is the Christian faith. You are asked three questions which summarise what Christians believe about God the Father, Jesus, and the Holy Spirit.

A RELATIONSHIP WITH GOD

The answer to each of these questions needs to be, '*I believe and trust in him.*' This is very important. As we saw earlier when thinking about what it means to believe in a doctor, it's not enough to *believe* in God simply in the sense of agreeing that he exists. There needs also to be the element of *trust*, of relationship, of commitment. Not just knowing *about* him, but also actually knowing him, personally.

This emphasises the way in which Christianity is not primarily a religious club or a set of rules telling us how to live our lives. It's first and foremost a lifelong *relationship* with God. This is the main thing that God is interested in: that we should *love* him and one another. To do this we need to spend time getting to know him better through daily prayer and reading the Bible. We need to let it be known that we love and trust him by the way we live and the things we say. For, as Jesus put it once when talking to his close followers, 'If anyone loves me, he will obey my teaching. My Father will love him, and we will come to him and make our home with him.'

THE BAPTISM ITSELF

You hand the baby over to the minister who may ask you to state his or her full name. Then, addressing baby by name, he will sprinkle water over his or her head, saying, '*I baptize you in the name of the Father, and of the Son, and of the Holy Spirit.*' Parents and godparents answer '*Amen*' to signify their agreement with what is going on. And so your baby becomes the latest in a long line stretching back nearly two thousand years.

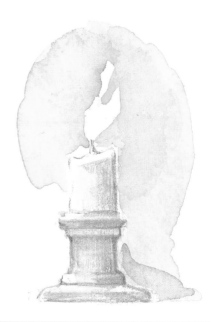

57 The priest or other person may give to a parent or godparent for each child A LIGHTED CANDLE, saying to each

> Receive this light.

And when a candle has been given to each one, he says

> This is to show that you have passed from darkness to light.

All **Shine as a light in the world**
to the glory of God the Father.

THE WELCOME

58 The priest and the congregation, representing the whole Church, welcome the newly baptized.

Priest God has received you by baptism into his Church.
All **We welcome you into the Lord's Family.**
We are members together of the body of Christ;
we are children of the same heavenly Father;
we are inheritors together of the kingdom of God.
We welcome you.

SWITCHED ON ...

The best antidote to darkness is light. And so light is a very powerful symbol of what happens when someone becomes a Christian. As Paul puts it in his New Testament letter to the Colossians, God 'has rescued us from the dominion of darkness and brought us into the kingdom of the Son he loves ...' A kingdom characterised by light and truth, freedom and justice. This transfer is symbolised by the giving of a lighted candle to a parent or godparent with the words, *'This is to show that you have passed from darkness to light.'*

But there's more. For us personally to cross over from darkness to light isn't the end of the story. The followers of Jesus are given the responsibility to help others to cross over too. This is the emphasis behind the congregation's reply: *'Shine as a light in the world to the glory of God the Father.'* Our job is to overcome the darkness around us with the light we have received. This echoes something Jesus said to his followers which is quoted in Matthew's Gospel: 'You are the light of the world. A city on a hill cannot be hidden. Neither do people light a lamp and put it under a bowl. Instead they put it on its stand, and it gives light to everyone in the house. In the same way, let your light shine before men, that they may see your good deeds and praise your Father in heaven.'

... AND PLUGGED IN!

This part of the service ends with the welcome from the congregation. We all join together in welcoming the latest member of the fastest-growing family in the world! Congratulations!

THE PRAYERS

59   Priest   Lord God our Father, maker of heaven and earth, we thank you that by your Holy Spirit *these children have* been born again into new life, adopted for your own, and received into the fellowship of your Church: grant that *they* may grow in the faith into which *they have* been baptized, that *they* may profess it for *themselves* when *they come* to be confirmed, and that all things belonging to the Spirit may live and grow in *them*. **Amen**.

60   Priest   Heavenly Father, we pray for the parents of *these children*; give them the spirit of wisdom and love, that their *homes* may reflect the joy of your eternal kingdom. **Amen**.

61   Priest   Almighty God, we thank you for our fellowship in the household of faith with all those who have been baptized in your name. Keep us faithful to our baptism, and so make us ready for that day when the whole creation shall be made perfect in your Son, our Saviour Jesus Christ. **Amen**.

62   Priest   Jesus taught us to call God our Father,
                   and so in faith and trust we say

All		*or*	
Our Father in heaven,			**Our Father, who art in heaven,**
hallowed be your name,			**hallowed be thy name;**
your kingdom come,			**thy kingdom come;**
your will be done,			**thy will be done;**
on earth as in heaven.			**on earth as it is in heaven.**
Give us today our daily bread.			**Give us this day our daily bread.**
Forgive us our sins			**And forgive us our trespasses,**
as we forgive those			**as we forgive those**
who sin against us.			**who trespass against us.**
Lead us not into temptation			**And lead us not into temptation;**
but deliver us from evil.			**but deliver us from evil.**
For the kingdom, the power,			**For thine is the kingdom,**
and the glory are yours			**the power, and the glory,**
now and for ever. Amen.			**for ever and ever. Amen.**

63   Priest   The grace of our Lord Jesus Christ, and the love of God, and the fellowship of the Holy Spirit be with us all evermore. **Amen**.

PRAYERS FOR PARENTS
AND GODPARENTS

The prayers which God hears most clearly are those which come from your heart. You don't need to be good with words - just tell God how you feel. But here are a few suggested prayers you could use as a framework for your own.

God our Father,
in giving us *this child*
you have shown us your love.
Help us to be trustworthy parents.
Make us patient and understanding,
that our *child* may always be sure of our love
and grow up to be happy and responsible;
through Jesus Christ our Lord. Amen.
(from *The Alternative Service Book*)

Dear Father, we give you thanks for children, and particularly for those who are committed to our care. We thank you for their innocence, their laughter, their loving, and their unquestioning trust in us. Help us, Lord, by word and deed to give them a simple and steadfast faith, a loving heart and a cheerful nature, that they may be equipped to be citizens of this world and the next, through Jesus Christ our Lord. Amen.
(from *More Prayers for Today's Church*)

Heavenly Father,
whose blessed Son shared at Nazareth
the life of an earthly home:
bless our home
and help all of us in this family
to live together in your love.
Teach us to serve you and each other,
and make us always ready to show your love to those in need;
for the sake of Jesus Christ our Lord. Amen.
(adapted from *The Alternative Service Book*)

Almighty God,
our heavenly Father,
who gave marriage to be a source of blessing to mankind,
we thank you for the joys of family life.
May we know your peace and presence in our home;
fill it with your love,
and use it for your glory;
through Jesus Christ our Lord. Amen.
(adapted from *The Alternative Service Book*)

A Record

....

CHILD OF

....

&

....

BORN ON

....

WAS BAPTISED
IN THE NAME OF THE FATHER,
AND OF THE SON,
AND OF THE HOLY SPIRIT

of the Day

ON

AT

BY

THE GODPARENTS ARE

FURTHER READING

On baptism

Baptism, Michael Green (Hodder & Stoughton, 1987)

On confirmation

Your Confirmation, John Stott (Hodder & Stoughton, 1991)
Being Confirmed, Nick Aiken (Marshalls, 1991)
Going On, John B. Taylor (Daybreak, 1989)
To Be Confirmed, Gavin Reid (Hodder & Stoughton, 1977)

On being a godparent

Godparents, Anne Watson (Kingsway, 1989)

On exploring Christianity

Explaining Your Faith, Alister McGrath (IVP, 1988)
Mere Christianity, C. S. Lewis (Fontana, 1952)
Questions of Life, Nicky Gumbel (Kingsway, 1993)
Is Anyone There? David Watson (Hodder & Stoughton, 1979)
Basic Christianity, John Stott (IVP, 1971)
What's the Point? Norman Warren (Lion, 1986)
Journey into Life, Norman Warren (Kingsway, 1980)
Why Jesus? Nicky Gumbel (Kingsway, 1991)

On reading the Bible

The Bible from Scratch, Simon Jenkins (Lion, 1987)
The Bible in Outline, John Balchin and others (Scripture Union, 1985)
Uncage the Lion, ed. Becky Totterdell (Scripture Union/Spring Harvest, 1990)
The Bible User's Manual, J. Balchin, D. Field and T. Longman (IVP, 1991)

On prayer

Don't Just Stand There ... Pray Something, Ronald Dunn (Scripture Press, 1992)
Listening to God, Joyce Huggett (Hodder & Stoughton, 1986)
Too Busy Not To Pray, Bill Hybels (IVP, 1988)
People in Prayer, John White (IVP, 1977)

On living as a Christian

New Life, New Lifestyle, Michael Green (Hodder & Stoughton, 1991)
Discipleship, David Watson (Hodder & Stoughton, 1981)
The Contemporary Christian, John Stott (IVP, 1992)
The Fight, John White (IVP, 1977)

On marriage

Journey into Marriage, Yvonne Warren (Kingsway, 1993)
Two into One, Joyce Huggett (IVP, 1989)

On bringing up children

How To Really Love Your Child, Ross Campbell (Scripture Press, 1987)
How To Really Know Your Child, Ross Campbell (Scripture Press, 1988)
Families on the Way, Carl Whitehouse (Scripture Union, 1989)
And Then I Had Kids, Susan Yates (Word, 1992)
Childhood Prayers and Verses, Carolyn Martin (Hodder & Stoughton, 1992)
Parents in Pain, John White (IVP, 1980)